Revised

Living With Children

New Methods for Parents and Teachers

Gerald R. Patterson, Ph.D.

Research Press
2612 North Mattis Avenue • Champaign, Illinois 61820

Contents

Acknowledgments

After 10 years of useful service, it is time to rewrite some of the sections from *Living With Children*. We approach the task with a good deal of reservation; it's something like being asked to alter an old friend. However, our experience in working with over 100 families of problem children showed that some of our earlier guesses must be changed. These people patiently applied the social learning concepts *and* provided corrective feedback to us. It is to these families that we owe a special debt of gratitude.

In the last 5 years, the Social Learning Project has worked with about 50 parents of normal preschool children. The reports of this work are forthcoming (Forgatch & Toobert, in preparation). This group taught us that while a book *may be* helpful for parents of problem children, there was a need for some very different material for parents of normal children. What was needed were *brief, very specific* instructions on how to change behaviors encountered by almost every parent. To meet this need, a whole new section has been added. Again, we owe a special debt to those parents who took the time to teach us what we needed to know.

The ideas expressed here are based upon social learning concepts from the work of B. F. Skinner (1953) and A. Bandura (1971). The specifics, however, arose from discussions with colleagues such as W. Bricker, J. Cobb, H. Hops, F. Kanfer, R. Littman, R. Ray, J. Reid, D. Shaw, K. Skindrud, J. Straughan, R. Weiss, R. Ziller, and many others.

There is perhaps one more debt which must be acknowledged and that is to the astonishing number of people who found the earlier version useful. This enduring interest places a special responsibility upon us to keep the material and approach up to date.

G. R. Patterson
Eugene, Oregon
June 1976

Introduction

For over a decade investigators working at Universities in Kansas, Stanford, Illinois, Oregon, Calgary, New York at Stony Brook, Michigan State, Vermont, Southern Illinois, and Tennessee have been developing a set of notions about how children learn to become people. Part of the work was devoted to training parents to change several aggressive, hyperactive, and stealing behaviors (Tavormina, 1974). Much of the recent effort has been to understand how to facilitate the development of normal child behaviors. Both developments are summarized in this revision of *Living With Children*.

The book is intended to assist parents of normal and problem children to deal with the situations that come up in *any* family. The general idea is certainly *not new*. Social learning theories underline the fact that *people teach people*. Section 1 of this book will help you to understand *how* that works. Sections 2, 3 and 4 will provide specific instructions on *what* to do about it. How can you help your child change his behavior? How is it that a child only three feet tall can reduce a grown woman to tears, causing her to scold and spank? How does a six-year-old boy train his father to yell at him? How do you train your four-year-old to mind? How do you get a child to go to bed on time (without nagging)?

Sure, these are all *simple* things. They are a small part of living together, but a significant part. What can parents do when things get way out of alignment, when they are trying to live with a real problem child? This book is about that, too; but certainly you would want to seek out professional assistance in using the ideas in this book to help such a child.

It has been our experience that parents of normal children can lift many of the procedures directly from the book and use them to teach the child to reduce the number of temper tantrums, to go to bed on time, to mind, etc. However, the ideas do not work for everyone; when they do not, then you would be wise to seek professional help.

This book has been written for parents who are not great readers of books. Some parents like to have their ideas laid out in a straightforward manner. This volume is written for them. For those who like more detail, more examples, and more about the theory, then *Families* (Patterson, 1971, 1975) would be the better choice.

Our experiences with parents have taught us that some ideas and approaches are difficult to put into words. They can be acted out better than they can be talked about. For example, the ideas of positive reinforcement and Time Out are terribly hard to write about. For this reason, cassette tapes have been developed which provide clear examples of how to do these things (Patterson & Forgatch, 1975, 1976).

It would seem time now to require that ideas about families be evaluated *before* they are presented to the public. Helping your child is simply too important a process to rely upon fads. Thus many of the ideas and procedures described here have been researched by *a number* of investigators. Since this work is far from being completed, wherever possible it will be referenced so that the parent or professional can determine for themselves how well documented a particular point really is. The fact that this evaluation continues means, of course, that this book will have to be revised yet again within a few years.

How to Use This Book

This book is designed to help you understand situations in which you or your child behaves in a way that is distressing to you. The book is written in the form of programmed instruction. This is a special kind of writing that makes it easier for the reader to learn. All of the main ideas in the book have been broken down into small units or items. You are asked to *respond actively* to these items, rather than to merely read them. For each of these units you will write an answer. You will then be able to check each answer immediately with the one provided at the end of the chapter.

This is not a test. It is the most efficient way for you to learn the main outlines of a social learning process. The questions are planned to encourage you to supply the right answer, because making correct responses helps you to remember and to learn.

Read each statement carefully. Write what you think belongs in the blank space in the book. The words at the end of each chapter are our suggested answers to each of the items. After you have written your answer, compare it with the one provided in the book. If your response is different, think about the difference in the meaning. Do not erase, but write the suggested response beneath yours. They may mean the same thing. Then continue with the next item.

Section 1
How Parents and Children Learn

It is hoped that this book will provide a guide for better understanding of the behavior of both parent and child. Section 1 tells "how it works." Parents need to do more than just "understand"; they need to know how to change what is going on in their families. Sections 2, 3 and 4 will tell what to do.

Even after 10 years of trying it out, it *still* seems like a good idea to teach parents what the mysterious process is about. How *do* family members go about the business of changing each other? My hunch is that once you know about it, you can figure out for yourself what to do. If not, the specific steps will come in later sections of the book. Those who don't want to bother with the business of knowing can skip to those sections right now and return to this section later. Of course, having once been a professor, I still feel that parents *ought to understand* these things. So . . . .

1
Social Learning

1. Most of what we see other people doing represents something they have learned. Talking, dressing, playing, and working at tasks are all things that are learned. It is also true that whining, fighting, or temper tantrums are _____ .

2. We believe that a child acts the way he does, not because he was born that way, but because he was _____ to behave that way.

By the time we are adults, we have learned an enormous number of things. We learn how to talk with our friends about the weather, politics, and the price of furniture. Throughout our lives, we are constantly learning how to respond to other people.

3. People, whether they realize it or not, are teaching each other all the time. They actually *change* each other. Psychologists use the term "social learning" to describe the ways people te_____ or ch_____each other.

4. Scolding and spanking are things that most parents learn to do at one time or another. It is also true that kissing, praising, and hugging are things that parents ＿＿＿＿＿ to do.

5. This means that a child who has been taught to misbehave can also be taught to ＿＿＿＿＿ .

6. This does not mean that a parent deliberately tries to teach a child to be bad. But many of the things parents say and do have unexpected results. Even the most well meaning parent can ＿＿＿＿＿ a child to misbehave.

7. It also means that if he has not yet learned to pick up his clothes, that he can be ＿＿＿＿＿ to do that, too.

The main idea is that children *and* parents *can change.* First, we need to understand *how* all these different things can be taught by family members. For example, how is it that a parent can be taught to scold and punish, or even to "love too much"?

Answer Key

1. learned
2. taught
3. teach
   change
4. learn
5. behave
6. teach
7. taught

2
What Are Reinforcers?

1. One of the most important things involved in this kind of learn-
    ing is something that parents have known for hundreds of
    years, but it has seldom been used very well. This first, simple
    idea involves the use of rewards or positive reinforcers. As we
    use the words here, a reinforcer and a _____ are
    about the same thing.

2. Giving the child a quarter as soon as he finishes mowing the
    lawn would be an example of using a reinforcer. If you gave
    him a piece of cake as soon as he cleaned his room, the positive
    reinforcer in this instance would be the piece of _____.

3. Food and money are not the only important rewards. In fact,
    many other kinds of reinforcers are far more useful. One of
    the most powerful reinforcers for a child is the love, interest,
    and attention from his mother and father. Listening to the
    child, hugging him, smiling at him, or talking to him are all
    _____, the kind that are given hundreds of
    times *every day* to most children.

4. When you are talking, your friends reinforce you by being good listeners. In this case, their listening is a positive reinforcer. If they stopped listening to you, you would probably _____ talking, or change the subject. If they did this to you very often, you would probably find new friends. In your next conversation with a friend, try looking out of the window and see what happens.

5. It is the people who provide a great deal of positive reinforcement for us that we generally choose as friends (Rosenfeld, 1966, 1967). Each friend teaches you what to talk to him about. He does this by being interested in only some of the things you talk about and not in others. If you talk about something that interests him, he listens closely; otherwise he becomes bored. His listening is a powerful _____ for your talking about that particular topic.

6. The next idea is that behavior followed by a positive reinforcer will occur more frequently in the future. If Karl's mother praised him each time he put his toys away, it is more likely that Karl will put his _____ away in the future.

7. Mother's reinforcement just this *one time* does not make it certain that Karl is going to put his toys away the next time. To *really* teach him to put away the toys, his mother would have to remember to reinforce him for this action _____ times. That means you must really work to change behavior. It requires *dozens* of reinforcers. Some parents simply don't have the time or energy to do it.

8. OK, how do you start? Suppose you wish your daughter would hang up her coat as soon as she takes it off. You can begin

teaching her by first telling her to hang up her coat and then giving her a positive _____ when she does it. There are many rewards you could use in such a situation. For example, you could simply smile and say "Thank you." Or you could give her a hug. All of these are positive reinforcers that you can use to teach your child.

This means that if you decide you want some changes in your family, you must first change the way in which you use your reinforcers. You should also assume that at first nothing will happen. It takes time. You have to plan ahead. But clearly *you* are the agent of change. The question is: "Are you any good at it?"

9. If Mother reinforces both Peggy and Dad by telling them she likes or appreciates their hanging up their coats, then they both will probably _____ their coats more often in the future. That sounds simple enough. But the difficult thing is to be consistent and continue reinforcing the desired behaviors. For example, it is hard to remember to tell your child (or husband) that you appreciate his hanging up his coat. The problem is that *most of us tend to take desirable behavior for granted* rather than remembering to _____ it.

If a response isn't reinforced once in awhile, even after it is learned, it is likely to weaken and perhaps disappear. This means that positive reinforcers are necessary not only to teach a person new behaviors but also to maintain those he already has.

10. Don't take your child's good behaviors for granted. Remember to _____ him once in awhile.

11. When an infant cries and is picked up, he is being taught to cry. The reinforcer for his crying is _____ .

12. While sitting at the table, one of the children begins to laugh when the baby smears potatoes all over his face. The child then puts more potatoes on his face and also some on the child sitting next to him. Now everybody is laughing and saying how cute he is. The family is accidentally _____ the baby for being messy.

13. These examples of a baby crying and a young child smearing food are not anything that is terribly serious. They are, however, examples of how normal families accidentally teach _____ behaviors to children.

14. Sometimes it is very difficult *not* to reinforce undesirable behaviors. In the morning you are in a hurry to get Johnny to school. He can't find his clothes. He doesn't button his shirt properly. Even though he is old enough to dress himself, you are really in a hurry that morning, so you help him to get ready. In doing so, you are reinforcing his being _____ .

15. The reinforcer for his not dressing himself was your help and attention. If you did this many times, you would be _____ him to be helpless.

16. You may have the same kind of problem when getting your family ready to go on a trip. In order to have everybody all set to leave on time, you end up doing everything for everyone. You are making it very probable that on the next trip you will have to work even _____ to get everybody ready.

17. You don't want your family to be so helpless, but you may
    have actually _____ them for being that way.

18. To change a situation like this one, or Johnny's, you might
    (for example) pick a time when you do not have a schedule to
    meet and announce "Today you get dressed all by yourself. As
    soon as you are dressed, you can go outside (or turn on TV)."
    In this way, the child is being reinforced for _____
    behaviors.

19. Although crying, smearing, and helplessness are not very seri-
    ous, they raise the question: "How can you weaken these be-
    haviors once they get started?" Parents frequently try spank-
    ing a child when he smears, cries, or dawdles. Spanking may
    work. However, there is a simpler way. In the example of the
    child who smeared potatoes, his family should be taught not
    to _____ the undesirable behavior.

20. As a second part of the same "learning" program, parents
    should also remember to reinforce a child's _____
    table manners.

21. If a response is never reinforced, it will be weakened. If a
    young child worked very hard keeping his room straight and
    no one ever commented on or noticed his efforts, then it is
    very likely that this behavior would be _____ .

22. If all the family stopped laughing at the baby when he smeared
    food, the action would eventually _____ .

11

23.   Each morning on your way to work you see an elderly man working in his garden. You say "Good morning." He never looks up or says anything to you. After several days of this you would probably _____ speaking to him every morning.

24.   Every morning Mr. Brown reads the paper while he eats breakfast. He doesn't talk while he is reading the paper. Everyone in the family learns not to talk to him at that time. He taught them this by simply not _____ them if they tried to start a conversation.

25.   As most parents know, punishment is another way of weakening behavior. If you spank, slap, or threaten your child, she will stop doing whatever bothers you—at least she will stop it for a little while. _____ and not reinforcing are *both* ways to *weaken behavior*.

Some parents use spankings and scolding very effectively. However, people in these families often feel angry and upset. In a later section of the book we will describe some punishments that are more effective than spankings, putdowns, or scoldings.

26.   So far we have stressed two main ideas: to _____ a behavior, you must reinforce it; to weaken a behavior, do not _____ it.

Answer Key

1. reward
2. cake
3. reinforcers
4. stop
5. reinforcer
6. toys
7. many
8. reinforcer
9. hang up
   reinforce *or* reward
10. reinforce *or* reward
11. being picked up
12. reinforcing
13. undesirable *or* inappropriate
14. helpless *or* dependent *or* immature
15. teaching *or* training
16. harder
17. reinforced *or* rewarded
18. desirable
19. reinforce *or* laugh at
20. desirable *or* good
21. weakened
22. weaken *or* stop
23. stop
24. reinforcing *or* answering *or* talking to
25. punishing
26. strengthen
    reinforce *or* reward

3
How Can We Use Reinforcers?

There are many things that can serve as positive reinforcers for most children. For example, listening, hugging, praise, a smile, or a kiss are all powerful rewards. Objects such as candy and toys are also examples of reinforcers that can be used to strengthen behavior.

1. For the child, *immediate* rewards are the most effective. The most common mistake parents make in using reinforcers is waiting too long after the child has acted before they get around to reinforcing him. To use rewards most effectively, the parent should reinforce a child _____ after he shows the desired behavior.

2. One mother waits 5 minutes to tell her son that she appreciated his hanging up his coat. A second mother reinforces her son 2 seconds after he hangs up his coat. The boy most likely to hang up his coat in the future is the one who was reinforced after _____ _____.

3. The second problem many parents have in using reinforcers is that they tend to take desirable behaviors for granted. Desirable behaviors should not be taken for granted, they should be

_____ .

4. Particularly when a child is first learning, he must be reinforced *often*. For example, when you are teaching him to wash his face, it might be wise to reinforce him *every time*. You might do this by saying, "Thank you for _____ your _____." At first, washing his face is not a duty, it is something you are teaching him.

5. In the beginning, the most effective way to teach him is to reinforce him _____ time he washes his face.

6. Also remember to reinforce him as _____ as possible after he washes it.

7. Many of the things we wish to teach a child are much more complicated than hanging up his coat or washing his face. For example, how do you teach a child to be "polite" or "to be a good student"? First, it is necessary to understand that "being a good student" is the last in a long series of steps. As a parent who wishes to teach your child to be a good student, it is necessary for you to figure out what these steps would be. You must also decide how you will reinforce him as he works on each of the _____ toward being a good student.

8. Most complicated social behaviors can be broken down into small steps. One of the goals of this book is to teach parents how to reinforce a child as he works on each of these smaller

steps. Many parents seem to want to wait until the child has climbed the whole mountain before they will get around to giving him a _____ .

9. There are hundreds of small steps involved in learning to be a "good child" or a "good student." When learning a new behavior, the reinforcer should be given for each of the _____ steps along the way rather than as a prize at the very end.

10. Suppose the teacher says that your son, Bill, is not a very good student, or that he is an "underachiever." What can you as a parent do about it?

    As a parent you have three problems to work out. First, how can you break the problem down into small steps? Next, how are you going to reinforce Bill as quickly as possible? Third, what kind of _____ will you use for completing each step?

11. You might begin by getting Bill to talk to you about school. Many parents make the mistake of asking their children about school and then when the child starts to tell them about it, they do not listen. In other words, they ask for the behavior and then they do _____ reinforce it when it occurs.

12. You might begin by setting aside 10 minutes each night during supper when Bill is encouraged to tell about school. His parents or other members of the family must actually *listen* and *talk* to him about doing better work at school. Their _____ and their _____ to him about experiences at school would be powerful reinforcers for him.

13. A second step would be to get Bill to start studying at home. You might reinforce him on the first night if he could work for just 10 minutes. In this situation _____ minutes of studying would represent a small first step toward the goal of being a better student.

14. It may be that Bill cannot sit still and work for 10 minutes. In that case, it is clear that the step is too _____ and should be shortened to just 5 minutes. The size of the step depends on the task and the child. Select a beginning point that is right for your child.

15. In this way the child is receiving reinforcement from the very first step of the program. As he goes along, the steps will become larger and he will have to do more work to get the same amount of reinforcement. He must work to obtain reinforcement, but it is your job as a parent to make it possible for him to be reinforced after each _____ along the way.

16. By the end of the first week, you might reinforce Bill only if he works 15 or 20 minutes. At the end of such a session you could reinforce him by asking him about the material he studied, and _____ while he talks about it.

17. Listening to him talk about his work or going over the work sheet with him would both be reinforcers. Remember that while you are reinforcing Bill you should not criticize him or his work. Sarcastically telling him that his work is "sloppy," for instance, would not _____ the behavior of studying.

18. Teaching him to sit still and work for 10 minutes is the first step, and that is all that he needs to do in order to get the reinforcement from you. A much later step might be to teach him to be neat or accurate in his work. Go one step at a time and use punishment as little as possible. If the child is trying, then _____ him for whatever step he is able to make.

19. If Bill's parents criticize or ridicule him at the first step because his work is not perfect, this will_____ the studying behavior.

20. Some parents wait until their child brings his report card home and then reinforce him with money or approval for getting good grades. This is not a good way to teach a young child to pay attention at school. He has to wait too long to receive the _____and the steps he must take to earn the reinforcer are too _____ .

21. Earlier we said that to strengthen a new behavior a reinforcer must be given often, and given _____ after the response.

22. Now we are also saying that to teach a child a new behavior you must reinforce him for each _____ step along the way to whatever goal you are working toward.

23. One reason that "bribes" do not ordinarily work in teaching children is that parents make the steps required to earn the bribes too _____ .

24. Joey is told that if he "behaves" all week long, he will get a reward of one dollar. This probably will not work because he must first learn to behave for a whole hour, then a whole _____ , then a whole week.

25. Let's suppose a father says to his son, who is failing in school, "If you get a C in composition next month, I'll give you a dollar." It is unlikely that the reinforcer will be very effective because for many children it is too _____ a step from failure to a C.

26. It might be better to cash in the dollar bill for 100 pennies. The pennies could be used as reinforcers, and one penny could be given for each_____ the child makes in the desired direction.

27. Different people progress at different speeds. Small steps for one person might be either too large or too _____ for another person.

28. If a child stops working, you can assume that the steps are not the right size or the reinforcer is too weak. If the child acts bored, it probably means she is not receiving enough _____ for her effort.

29. For example, suppose you decide to improve Debbie's spelling. At first you might give her a penny for spelling a three-letter word correctly. Then she must learn a five-letter word to earn a penny. Debbie is now doing more work for the same amount of _____ .

30. This is a kind of "apprentice" system. When she begins, the apprentice receives her wages for very simple tasks. As she learns, she receives reinforcement (wages or praise) only for doing more _____ tasks.

31. For example, young Timmy sucks his thumb and you want to teach him to keep his thumb out of his mouth. The "steps" for this program could be increases in the amount of time that he can keep his thumb out of his mouth. The first _____ you reward might be "thumb out of mouth for 5 seconds."

32. During that first morning, each time Timmy is "without thumb" for 5 seconds you might say, "That's _____. You don't have your thumb in your mouth."

33. As your program moves along, you will notice that he sometimes leaves his thumb out of his mouth for 15 seconds. As this happens more often, begin to reinforce him only when he has his thumb out of his mouth for 15 seconds. In this second step, Timmy must achieve more to get the same

_____ .

34. Giving him a hug or a smile when you tell him how well he is doing at that time would add to the effectiveness of your

_____ .

35. As he moves along through these steps, you might add further reinforcement for Timmy's progress by announcing to the family at dinner that he kept his thumb out of his mouth for a whole hour that day. This would remind the family that they, too, can reinforce these behaviors. Teaching is more likely to be effective if all of the people in the family help carry out the reinforcement program. Training the child should be an affair in which the _____ family participates.

36. Now, let's summarize the points made in this section. Behaviors that are reinforced are _____.

37. If, when the child responds, the reinforcements do not occur, then the behavior is _____.

38. When a new behavior is being taught, reinforcements should be given _____ after the behavior occurs.

39. The reinforcements should be given at first for small steps and later for _____ steps.

40. Positive reinforcers are used differently early in the training program than they are when the child already has learned the desired behavior. For example, if you were beginning to teach a child to "mind," you would try to reinforce him_____ time he minds you.

41. However, once he begins to mind you fairly well, it would then be necessary to reinforce him only every third time. Later still, he might mind you several times without your reinforcing him for it. If you forget and never reinforce him for minding, that behavior will be _____ .

42. Studies show that once behaviors are learned they are more likely to last if the behavior is *not* reinforced every time. Reinforcing every time is important during the _____ stages of learning a behavior, but later on it is better if you reinforce the behavior only _____ .

43. The child who hangs up his coat regularly, even though his mother reinforces him for it only occasionally, is more likely to have a long-lasting habit than the child whose mother reinforces him _____ time he hangs up his coat.

Keep in mind, then, that what is done to get a behavior started requires *a lot* more effort from you than it will later on when the child is well along in the program.

Answer Key

1. immediately
2. two (2) seconds
3. reinforced
4. washing
   face
5. every *or* each
6. soon
7. steps
8. reinforcer *or* reward
9. small *or* many
10. reinforcer
11. not
12. listening
    talking
13. ten (10)
14. large *or* long
15. step
16. listen
17. strengthen *or* reinforce
18. reinforce
19. weaken
20. reinforcer *or* reward
    large *or* long
21. immediately *or* quickly
22. small
23. large *or* long
24. day
25. large
26. step
27. small
28. reinforcement
29. reinforcement
30. difficult
31. step
32. good *or* fine
33. reinforcement
34. reinforcement
35. whole *or* entire
36. strengthened
37. weakened
38. immediately
39. larger
40. every *or* each
41. weakened
42. early
    occasionally
43. every

24

4
Social and Nonsocial Reinforcers

1. Punishment is something you use sparingly. It teaches the child to stop doing something, but your real task as a parent is to teach him to be a person. To do that, you must teach him to do positive things. For this, you use reinforcers. Awarding food, money, love, or attention for behavior is positive reinforcement. A mother listening to her child is giving him a _____ reinforcer. A program means you have a plan. For example, a plan to increase some behavior. When doing this, *the reinforcer is given for some specific behavior.*

2. Food, money, candy, and toys are nonsocial reinforcers. Praise, smiles, approval, attention, and kisses are examples of social reinforcers. A pat on the back would be a _____ reinforcer if you were using it to strengthen a behavior such as coming to dinner on time.

3. Staring out of the window as your husband talks to you would not be a reinforcer for his talking. Smiling or laughing at the clever things he says could be a powerful s_____ r_____ .

4. The behavior being strengthened would be your husband's
   _____. Some wives say their husbands never talk
   to them. It probably means that the wife seldom

   _____ .

5. Both adults and children receive hundreds of these social
   reinforcers each day, but most people do not notice what it is
   that other people reinforce us for. Also, the changes in behavior are so slow that we don't notice they are happening. Most
   behaviors are learned as a result of watching other people and
   then getting s_____ r_____ for
   trying them out.

6. Social reinforcers are "small" events that happen to a child
   hundreds of times each day. Slowly, as a result of these events,
   the child acquires a "personality." Unless you learn to observe
   what it is that a child is being reinforced *for*, you will probably not understand how the child _____ that
   personality.

7. When you design a program for changing some child behaviors,
   you will certainly want to use social reinforcers. However, you
   can often speed up the change by adding some non_____
   reinforcers, such as money, candy, toys, or "points." This is
   especially true if you, as a parent, are working with a severe
   problem child. At that point, the use of nonsocial reinforcers
   becomes crucial. A later section of the book shows how to do
   that. But even a normal child will enjoy working for something. It is like being an adult and working for a salary.

8. Another kind of nonsocial reinforcer that has worked well is the "point system." In this method, the child earns points (which mother, or child, writes down). Later, the child trades in his points for money, toys, or something important to him. Earning 500 _____ for a fishing trip might be a goal in a child's point system.

9. The child receives a point immediately following the desired behavior. For example, when he washes his face, his mother _____ records the point in his notebook.

10. The parents and a younger child might decide that when he has earned 100 points he can buy a model airplane. In this system, each point is a _____ .

11. Tell your child when you make such a mark. You might say "That was good. I'll mark another _____in your book."

12. At the end of the day, tell him how many points he has earned, especially if he is a young child or has never been on a program before. Be sure that he knows what he is earning with the _____ .

13. Be sure that you are always using both social and nonsocial _____ to strengthen self-helping behavior. Your praise and approval are of great importance to young children. Use them often. You should be *praising* your child *at least several times a day,* for example, "You look nice." "That was a good job, thank you." Some parents feel that praising a child will make him weak. This is just not true.

14. When beginning a program, the first few days' points may be worth a penny each. Later, it may take 3 or 4 to earn one _____ .

15. This procedure can be rather flexible because parents and child can change the system from one week to the next. One week he may be earning pennies, another week he may be earning points to go on a trip with his father. What the points will earn is up to the _____ and the child. In this way, a good retraining program is tailor-made for the individual child and his family.

16. Once the child is doing well on a new behavior, you might fade the points out and continue to use just social _____ . It is these things that keep his, and your, social behaviors going.

At this point you might start on a new program: "You did great on practicing minding. How would you like to earn points for cleaning up your room each day?"

Answer Key

1. positive
2. social
3. social reinforcer
4. talking
   listens *or* reinforces
5. social reinforcement
6. learned *or* developed
7. social
8. points
9. immediately
10. reinforcer
11. point
12. points
13. reinforcers
14. penny
15. parents
16. reinforcers

5
Children Train Parents

1. There is more to life than just positive reinforcers. There are things that happen in the life of adults and children that are painful. For example, electric shock, being pinched or bumped hard, being burned, being near a very loud noise, being yelled at or spanked. For most children, being scolded would be a _____ event.

2. A child runs through the house yelling and shouting. Mother is very tired and has a headache. She is lying down and trying to get some rest. Very likely, the child's yelling and screaming is also _____ to her.

3. Anything that will "turn off" a painful event is strengthened. Behaviors that turn off painful events are _____ .

4. Most of us learn to avoid or get away from _____ _____ .

5. Some things parents do to their children were learned and strengthened because they helped turn off painful events. For example, Mr. Harvey comes home tired. The children are being loud and noisy. He sits down and turns on the TV set, and then he can't hear the yelling any more. The behavior "turn on the TV" was _____ .

6. A response that is reinforced is more likely to occur again in the future. If a response is successful in turning off a painful event, that response will occur _____ frequently in the future.

7. That means that next time Mr. Harvey comes home tired and the children are being very noisy, the thing he is likely to do is to _____ _____ the TV.

8. Another thing the tired father might have done was to shout "Shut up," and threaten to slap the next noise maker. Often this works, and for a short time the children stop making noise. In this case, the children are _____ their father for shouting and threatening.

9. Next time the children make noise, the thing that this father is most likely to do is to yell _____ _____.

10. If this happened a number of times, the children would actually train the _____; but probably neither the father nor the children would be aware of this fact. Mr. Harvey may be thinking, "That'll teach those kids not to be so noisy!" But who is teaching whom?

11. Mrs. Moore is loud and bossy; she is nagging morning and evening. She seldom has a pleasant thing to say to anyone. Her husband manages to disappear every night—bowling, working, or going to meetings. For him, getting out of the home at night is strengthened because it turns off his wife's nagging. Mrs. Moore has _____ her husband to stay away from home.

12. The painful event being avoided in this kind of training would be the _____ .

13. The behavior that is reinforced because it turns off the nagging would be _____ .

14. Mrs. Moore is accidentally providing reinforcement for her husband's learning to _____ the house.

15. A behavior that helps you *avoid* something unpleasant is strengthened. For example, *not* going to the dentist's for a checkup is reinforced because it makes it possible for you to _____ an unpleasant situation.

16. Aunt Minnie complains all the time. Each time you see her she has new aches or at least a new medicine. She has few interests other than what is wrong with her own body. As much as you love Aunt Minnie, you find yourself going to visit her less and less often. Your behavior of not going to visit her is _____ by avoiding her discussion of her wayward bowels!

17. Leaving early would be another behavior that would be rein-
    forced when you visit Aunt Minnie. The behavior is strength-
    ened because it turns off an _____ event.

18. Turning off something _____ and giving a positive
    reinforcer are both important parts of the process of teaching
    social behaviors to children.

19. They both_____ behaviors.

20. Most parents will teach a child a social behavior and then rein-
    force him every once in a while when he does it right. How-
    ever, there are other parents who somehow "forget" to use
    positive reinforcers. In such a home, when a child behaves
    himself, his mother stops nagging or scolding. In this way he,
    too, is reinforced for learning desirable social behaviors. But
    his mother is trained so that she _____all of the time in-
    stead of using positive reinforcers.

21. Both positive reinforcers and punishment work in controlling
    behavior. But the use of pain and discomfort to teach a child
    social behaviors means that the parent must be always on her
    toes, ready to punish, scold, spank, and threaten for all of the
    small ways in which a child can get off base. Such a household
    would be a rather _____ place in which to live.

22. One of the interesting things about such a household is that
    the family has _____ the mother to behave this
    way.

23. When she yells loud enough or long enough, they do what she wants them to do. In summary, it is not just children who are taught by positive reinforcers and by avoiding discomfort. It is clear that, to some extent, children teach their_____ how to behave and how to run a family.

24. Another part of the process probably affects many mothers. A new mother works very hard taking care of the house and the babies. But nowadays there is very little social _____ for "being a good mother."

25. In earlier times, a grandmother or maiden aunt living in the home probably provided a good deal of _____ reinforcement for a young mother's efforts and successes. The relative usually helped with the work, too.

26. Everyone, children and adults alike, must receive a minimal amount of social reinforcement. If they do not, people are likely to feel somewhat depressed. The adult or child who receives little or no social reinforcement from anyone would eventually become a rather depressed individual. Many housewives are in this situation because they are provided with very little _____ _____ . The reason for this is that children do not often reinforce mothers; and husbands are often too busy with their jobs.

27. If the husband is preoccupied with his work and not particularly interested in babies, his wife is deprived of social reinforcers and begins to feel _____ .

28. When a mother is *not getting* much reinforcement, she is not likely to be able *to give* many social reinforcers to either her husband or her children. Then she will train them to change behaviors by making them want to ＿＿＿＿＿the pain and discomfort of her anger.

29. By screaming and shouting, she does influence the behavior of her husband and children. Gradually, however, she must use it so often that the other people in the family may begin to avoid *her.* She then gets even fewer ＿＿＿＿＿＿ ＿＿＿＿＿＿ .

30. As a result, she feels even more depressed and angry. In this unhappy situation the ＿＿＿＿＿＿ trains her family to avoid her. They in turn teach her to act like a fishwife.

31. If instead they give her a great deal of praise, it is a surprising, scientific fact that she will give it back. In fact, studies show that the person in the family who gives the most praise also ＿＿＿＿＿＿ the most.

The same thing holds true for pain. There, too, the person who gives the most gets the most. As a study of your own, try counting the number of times you praise your spouse or your child. For one day give three times that much and see what happens.

You do not use up the love supply by giving it to your family. Go ahead! You will get it all back!

Answer Key

1. painful
2. painful
3. strengthened *or* reinforced
4. painful events
5. learned *or* strengthened
6. more
7. turn on
8. reinforcing
9. "Shut up"
10. father
11. trained *or* taught
12. nagging
13. leaving, bowling, etc.
14. leave
15. avoid
16. reinforced *or* strengthened
17. unpleasant *or* painful
18. painful *or* unpleasant
19. strengthen *or* reinforce
20. nags *or* scolds
21. unpleasant *or* painful
22. trained *or* taught
23. parents
24. reinforcement
25. social
26. social reinforcement
27. neglected *or* depressed
28. avoid
29. social reinforcers
30. mother
31. receives *or* gets

6
Accidental Training and Dependency

1. This kind of training of parents by children and children by
    parents is largely *unplanned*. Most children do not intend to
    reinforce their mothers for scolding and nagging, and so on. On
    the other hand, most parents do not intend to _____
    their children for whining or for having temper tantrums or
    being afraid. People are usually not very much aware of what
    they teach each other.

    From observations made in the homes and classrooms, it seems
    that quite often parents accidentally reinforce their children for un-
    desirable behavior. Once parents become aware of which behaviors
    they want and learn how to reinforce those behaviors, then the un-
    desirable behaviors should decrease.

2. Even undesirable behavior that is followed by positive rein-
    forcers will be _____.

3. For example, Sally is playing with her brother. She wants the toy he is playing with. She whines and says "Give me that toy." Her brother doesn't give her the toy, so she whines louder. Mother gets upset about the noise and tells the brother to give Sally the toy. In this situation, Sally was being reinforced for _____ .

4. The reinforcer that Sally received was the _____ .

5. The reinforcer obtained by her mother was the "turning off" of the unpleasant event of Sally's _____ .

6. Our prediction would be that in the future, when things are not going the way Sally wants them to, she would _____ .

If we asked the mother why she was training her child to whine, she would undoubtedly say that she really didn't mean to do that.

7. Probably much of the training of children is done accidentally. The fact that a child has temper tantrums or some other undesirable behavior does *not* mean that she has "bad" parents who don't love her, or who spank too often, or who frustrate her too much. The child has temper tantrums because of poor _____ , not because of "disturbed parents."

8. Once you realize who does the reinforcing and when it occurs, it should be possible to weaken undesirable behaviors and to strengthen socially desirable behaviors. To make these changes,

you must first become aware of what the reinforcers are, and when and how often you use them to strengthen behaviors. The first step is to learn to _____ both your child and what you are doing.

There are other examples of accidental training. Training for helplessness is one that occurs often.

9. An infant must be dependent upon his environment because he is helpless. He cannot feed himself. As he grows, he becomes increasingly able to take care of himself. He learns to crawl and later to walk. He learns to talk and dress himself. However, some parents continue to reinforce their child for being _____.

10. He becomes so helpless that he depends upon the parents to do many things he could do himself. Imagine a seven-year-old child who cannot dress himself. When he asks his mother to tie his shoe for him, she does. This reinforces him for being helpless. As an alternative, she could teach him to _____ his own shoe.

11. Another form of dependent behavior involves always being "close" to mother. If the mother is in the kitchen, the child is in the kitchen. The helpless child may even sleep with his parents. If the mother is trying to talk to friends, this child is crawling over her lap, whining and interrupting. When he does, then his mother pays _____ to him. She is reinforcing him for making a nuisance of himself.

12. The parents are often convinced that if they could just "give" enough, he would grow out of it. He doesn't. And all their giving only further reinforces _____.

13. It is hard to say just why some parents reinforce dependent behavior. Some reinforce the child for being helpless because at an earlier time the child had a serious illness. When sick in bed, all of us are strongly reinforced for being_____ . Sometimes a mother will simply forget to stop "nursing" a child.

There are also parents who seem to teach their children to depend upon them in order to fill a need in their own lives. These people are terribly lonely and, in a sense, are actually training some-one to "lean" on them.

14. Some parents are just in too much of a hurry. Billy's mother works hard and has to leave home before it is time for him to go to school. Billy is slow. She has to dress him. She is forced to _____ him for being helpless. Even though he's a third-grader, he eats so slowly that she must feed him in the morning.

15. She doesn't want him to help her around the house because he always makes a mess. He can't even set the table without drop-ping something on the floor. After dinner she plays a game with him, reads to him, and puts him to bed. This child lives in a world where he has to do very little in order to be paid off. He is dressed, fed, and entertained by one person. The way his reinforcers are earned almost guarantees that he will con-tinue to be _____.

16. It is not surprising that when he faces some other environment where he must respond appropriately in order to be positively reinforced, he does not do well. When he is first taken to school, he is frightened. The fear is real. Being left with a baby-sitter can also make him _____ .

17. Fear, too, can be accidentally _____. There are several ways of doing it. Training a child to be extremely dependent is one way.

18. There are *several* ways of learning to be afraid. One way is to watch other people who are afraid. If there is a storm and children see that their mother is afraid, then they will probably be _____ of storms.

19. If a young girl sees her grandmother shriek and jump on a chair in obvious fright when a mouse runs across the room, it is very likely that the girl will learn to fear _____.

20. A parent who was frightened and tense when near water or out in the woods would almost certainly teach his child to be afraid in these situations. A number of research studies have shown that mothers who have many fears have children who have many of the same _____ .

21. Keep in mind that most of us learn to stop being afraid of many of these things. Fear, then, is a behavior that is_____ , and the child can be trained in such a way as to increase or decrease his fear.

22. The best accidental trainers in the family are the brothers and sisters. For example, one of them is using the bike and another thinks it is his turn to use it. After a short argument, he shoves her off and takes it. She cries, he gets the bike. What was the reinforcer? It was the _____ .

23. What was reinforced? It was_____.

24. As another example, one child is watching TV. The other wishes to look at another station. He yells, nothing happens. He yells louder and she changes the station. She reinforced him for _____ . What it also means is *more yelling in the future.*

25. Brothers and sisters teach each other to use pain control techniques. All the parent has to do is to let it happen. It is accidental training but you as a parent can _____ it.

26. Count the amount of whine, yell, tease, put downs, crying, or hits in your family. If behaviors like these total one per minute, you have let the accidental training go too far. The idea presented in this book is a very optimistic one. Things in your family may accidentally get shaped into uncomfortable patterns. However, you *can* change that. Social behaviors are taught; that means that they can be _____ . It is your responsibility as a parent to decide what, if anything, needs changing.

Answer Key

1. reinforce
2. strengthened
3. whining
4. toy
5. whining
6. whine
7. training
8. observe
9. helpless *or* dependent
10. tie
11. attention
12. helplessness
13. helpless *or* dependent
14. reinforce
15. dependent
16. afraid *or* frightened
17. taught *or* learned
18. afraid
19. mice
20. fears
21. learned
22. bike
23. pushing *or* taking what you want
24. yelling
25. change *or* stop
26. changed

Section 2
Changing Undesirable Behavior

The chapters that follow provide a more detailed description of children and families with extreme problem behaviors. These families were referred because of problems severe enough to require professional help. Obviously, many of their problems were more severe than those found in the average family. For this reason, the descriptions of these families may not be helpful to all readers. However, the problems discussed here can be found in most families, but in different degrees. Because these families were kind enough to permit observers to make extensive investigations in their homes, we were able to reconstruct some of the steps that were involved in the training of these problem children.

Each of the chapters represents a different family; each chapter also outlines the "treatment program" that was used in that case. The general approach was to teach the parents the principles of social learning, and then to work in the home demonstrating how these principles could be used to help that child and that family. In all cases, the parents were trained "to do" their own treatment; and most of these parents were successful in making major changes in the behavior of their children.

7
How to Observe and Count

1. *Before* you start a program, observe the behavior you wish to change. Use at least three days for this phase. The first step in changing a behavior is to _____ the behavior.

2. The first step in observing your child is to decide *what it is that you are going to look at.* For a child who is untidy you might, for example, actually count the articles of clothing or toys that he leaves lying about the house. For a child with a "bad temper" you might actually _____ the number of temper tantrums she has in a day.

3. As we use the words in this book, "observing" and "counting" are about the same. With something as important as your child's behavior, the task of changing it deserves your careful consideration. Teaching you to actually count the behaviors will help to make you a more careful observer. In order to count something, you must define and look at it _____ .

4. Before we can teach the "messy" child some new behaviors, we first count the things that he leaves lying about the house. At first just the parents will do the counting, but later in the program they might also train the child to count his own behavior. It is best to select one time during the day and do your counting at that time. After dinner you might walk through the house and count the things lying about. When you finish counting, write down the number. In 4 days of counting you will have _____ of these numbers written down.

5. If the child knows that he is being counted, it is often the case that it will affect the way he behaves. It is probably a good idea to tell him, "I want to help you practice not teasing your sister so much. Every time you tease, I'm going to put a mark right here." Do *not* lecture him. In no way communicate that he is a _____ boy.

6. Put the chart up in plain sight. Tape it to the refrigerator door. As you record, let the child know how he is doing, for example, "You're doing great, you only teased once all day!" Unless you are working on a severe problem child, count only _____ behavior at a time.

Behavior	Days						
	M	T	W	Th	F	S	S
Teasing	⌗⌗ II	⌗⌗ III	I				

The chart can be very simple, like this one.

7. After you have counted the behaviors for several days, you are ready to plan a program. You should also *continue to count* the behaviors *during* such a program. It is important at all stages of a program for changing "undesirable behaviors" that you actually _____ the behaviors.

8. Remember, too, that you can observe and count parental behaviors. For example, in some families the father seldom reinforces anyone. His wife and children can take time each day to _____ the number of positive reinforcers the father gives. Or, the behavior to be changed might be the nagging, scolding behavior of the mother. The father and children in that family could count these each day.

9. The reason for all this observing and counting is that behavior changes *slowly*. Also, unless you have data, it is easy to kid yourself about whether or not you are being effective. After you start your program, your chart should show some improvement within a few days. If not, then change your_____.

Answer Key

1. observe
2. count
3. carefully *or* closely
4. four (4)
5. bad
6. one (1)
7. count
8. count
9. program

8
Time Out: Punishment for Little People

Changing behavior with positive reinforcement is the best way. However, it moves along slowly. And there are some things children do that you need to change quickly, for example, hitting the baby or yelling in your ear when you talk on the telephone. Punishment, if it is used properly, will produce rapid changes in behaviors that disrupt the family.

1. The punishments used by most parents consist of nagging, scolding, and when really angry, they _____.

2. The problem is that most of the time scolding and yelling does _____ work. "You are a mean kid, now stop teasing your sister" may work for a minute or two and then they are back at it again. Even when it does work, people wind up feeling badly.

3. When you get angry, you try slapping or hitting. That stops the undesirable behavior but there are two things wrong with it: (1) both you and the child are likely to get upset for quite awhile; (2) you just can't hit the child _____ time he does the undesirable thing.

4. That is a problem because if he only is punished for the behavior once in a while, it can actually make things worse. When you decide to use punishment *to change* something your child does, figure on using it *every time,* especially at first. When you start a program for behavior change, *be consistent* or you may make things _____ .

5. Time Out (TO) is a punishment that really works. After a few days of practice, it can be used with neither the child nor the parent getting very upset. Generally it is useful only for younger children, ages three to eleven, or perhaps twelve. If you have an adolescent, do _____ try to put your older child in TO!

6. TO means Time Out from positive reinforcement. It requires a place where there are no toys, no other people, and nothing to play with. It should *not* be dark or frightening. The best place in the house is the bathroom. People have tried a chair in a corner or in the hallway, but usually these alternatives do *not* work. TO occurs best in the _____ .

7. Many people say "Sure, we did that and it didn't work." What it usually means is that they tried it once or twice, but they did not (1) use it every time, or (2) did not use the bathroom, or (3) made any one of the other errors which are easily made in the use of TO. Given a normal child, the proper use of TO will be effective in _____ behavior.

8. As a first step, select only one behavior that you are sure you wish to change, for example, not minding, whining, teasing, etc. Set up a positive reinforcement program for the behavior which you wish to take its place and announce to the child:

"You do a lot of nice things for me but I want to help you to practice not teasing more. From now on, each time you tease, I'm going to say 'That was a tease, go to Time Out.' What we do then is to go to the bathroom like this" (take him gently by the hand) "and you sit in there for 2 minutes. I'll set the timer (egg timer) for 2 minutes and put it outside by the door. OK, you sit there, I'll close the door, and set the timer. When it goes off, you come out."

For some young children or for severe problems, you might wish to place all towels, toilet articles, etc., in a box. Remove the box each time you use TO during the first few days. There are a number of rules to keep in mind. First, after you have decided to change the behavior, do *not* lecture or scold when it next happens. Simply say "OK, that was one, go to

_____.

9. When you first use it, the child may whine, run, argue, or simply refuse to go. *Be calm.* Say "OK, that is another minute," and ask again. After 2 or 3 refusals in a row, you might be tempted to drag him or carry him to his just reward. However, don't do that. Don't yell, don't argue, don't hit, and don't _____.

10. If he makes a mess, have him _____ it up immediately.

11. If he refuses to clean it up, then no lecture, no arguments about why he should, just set a consequence, for example, "OK, I'll clean it up but no TV for you today." If he runs out of the bathroom, kicks the door, yells, etc., then say "OK, that is one more minute." There is a _____ for *each thing* he does. If he does TO well, then tell him so. "That's a good boy, you did TO very well."

12. Research studies show that 3 minutes of Time Out work as well as 30 minutes. It is better for him if you use short time periods (2, 3, or 4 minutes). But whatever you start with, stay with that amount of time. *Do not start* at 15 minutes and then try to cut it down. TO is *not* revenge. Don't let yourself get angry and yell "OK, that's 100 minutes of TO," when you've been using only 3 minutes. Stay with the same amount and keep TO _____.

13. *Do not* argue with him while he is in TO or afterward about being fair. If you're concerned about this, then let your spouse or a friend observe you and let you know if you are using punishment too much. Some parents *do*. The first few days you may find yourself using TO a half dozen times for this *one* problem. It should taper off after a few days to one or _____ per day.

14. You can use delayed TO, too. If you are shopping and he does the problem behavior, then say "OK, when we get home you go right to TO!" Once you begin a program to change a behavior, remember to be consistent and to use TO _____ time the problem comes up.

TO sounds simple to use; it is not. If you have difficulty in using it, then you might listen to the extensive examples on the cassette tapes by Patterson and Forgatch (1975, 1976) or consult an expert. If you apply the procedures properly, then you should be yelling at your child less and spanking rarely.

Answer Key

1. spank *or* hit *or* slap
2. not
3. every *or* each
4. worse
5. not
6. bathroom
7. changing
8. Time Out
9. drag *or* use physical force
10. clean
11. consequence
12. short *or* brief *or* to three (3) minutes
13. two (2)
14. each *or* every

9
Retraining

This chapter is a review of some of the key ideas presented thus far. These are the ideas you will need to understand in order to change behavior.

1. There are two general ideas involved in retraining your child. The first part of your program is to weaken the undesirable behaviors; the second part, going on at the same time, is to strengthen a desirable behavior that will *compete* with the undesirable one. For example, if your child fights too much, you would try to weaken fighting and to _____ a competing behavior, such as "playing nicely," or "cooperating with other children."

2. Competing behaviors are those that cannot be done at the same time, such as sharing and grabbing. For each problem, then, it is up to you to think of a behavior that would replace it. For a child who won't mind, the _____ behavior might be cooperating.

3. For a child who cries and won't let mother out of his sight, the competing behavior might be playing by himself. Each time such a behavior occurs you might _____ it.

4. Your task is to find ways to_____ the undesirable behavior and to strengthen the_____ behaviors.

5. Let's suppose that your son has a temper tantrum in the supermarket because he wants an ice cream cone. If you buy the cone to turn off the behavior, it is more likely that he will have _____ _____ in stores in the future.

6. As noted earlier, one way of handling it is to put the child in Time Out (TO) when he returns home. That means TO after *every* _____ _____ .

7. In building a program to change this, you would also want to strengthen something to take the place of the temper tantrums. Reward him or put a gold star on his chart (see page 70) each time he can go to the store and be a "big boy," for example, no _____ _____ .

8. Remember that you are not going to change behavior in a single trial. It might take you a dozen temper tantrums for which you put him in TO before you notice any change on his _____ _____ graph.

9. This means that you must *be consistent.* When a temper tantrum occurs, no matter what the situation, provide no reinforcement. Once you begin a program, if you "give in" and reinforce the undesirable behavior, it is even more powerful than when you began. Once you start a TO program, be

_____.

10. Once again, remember to use positive social reinforcers for behaviors that will compete with temper tantrums. For example, each time he walks through the supermarket without having a tantrum, you might _____ him or _____ him.

11. You might also announce to the rest of the family that night what a "big step" Johnny took that day in not having his regular temper tantrums. This will provide additional positive social reinforcers for behaviors that compete with

_____ _____.

12. At the beginning of your program, try to think of the competing desirable behavior as "new"; that is, a behavior that should be reinforced very often, and as quickly as possible. You might even think up situations in which he could try out the new behaviors. In other words, you might take him to 2 or 3 stores in one morning. Your success in this kind of program depends partly on your thinking up ways in which your child can practice the "new" behaviors (and be reinforced) many, many times. Keep in mind that reinforcers must be given to him _____ times before you can expect the behavior to be strengthened very much.

13. As you begin to learn how to help your child, it is best to begin with something very simple. For example, teach your child to come to the table with clean hands before you tackle something as complex as helping him get better grades. Start with _____ behaviors first.

14. Behavior may change slowly. Do not expect the program to work until you have tried it for a number of days. For example, some children have to be placed in TO 30 or 40 times before they stop hitting their brothers and sisters. You might also give 50 to 100 reinforcers before the new behavior is _____ enough to replace the unwanted behavior.

15. By counting the behavior, you can *see* the changes going on—*slowly*—day by day. Do not be impatient, but remember to keep the steps small so that he always earns a great deal of reinforcement as he changes. For example, if you are reinforcing him for picking up his clothes, you might at first give him a "point" for picking up his clothes just in the living room each day. If he is successful, you would tell him how pleased you are *and* give him a point. Using a combination of _____ and _____ reinforcers will be more effective in strengthening the desired behavior.

16. After several days of this, *if he has been successful,* you might tell him he has been doing so well that now he can earn even more points. If he cleans up both the living room and his bedroom, he will get twice as many points. After the third or fourth day, you might add another area of the house as another step. Make sure that he has been successful on one step before going on to another. And make sure that he gets a lot of _____ for each successful step.

17. When you think he is earning enough points each day, you might increase the amount of work that he has to do in order to earn the same number of points. How quickly you increase either points or work is up to the child. If your graph shows that he is no longer improving, then you should increase the amount of reinforcers *or* make the steps smaller. If behavior doesn't change, it is a bad program. When this happens, change the _____ .

18. Behavior may also stop improving because the child will tire of one type of reinforcer after a few days, such as candy. This simply means that you must change reinforcers. For example, you might try _____ or change the menu often.

19. In summary, before you begin to change a defined behavior, you must first observe and _____ it.

20. Then, carefully plan the manner in which you can weaken the undesirable behavior, and the steps you can take in _____ a competing, desirable one. Be sure both parents discuss this before you begin.

21. Throughout the program you must remember to use social reinforcers along with the nonsocial reinforcers. Once you begin to see changes in behavior, it is generally possible to decrease the nonsocial reinforcers. This means that you are more likely to use things like candy, points, and money at the beginning than at the _____ of the program.

22. After real improvement has occurred, you can gradually reduce the amount of toys, candy, or money being earned, but actually increase the amount of social reinforcers. In this way, _____ _____ become the most important ones for *maintaining* the new behaviors. These changes should be brought about gradually.

23. It is also true that simply reading a book of this kind will not make you a professional child psychologist. If you have serious problems with your child, you should seek professional advice. Even with relatively minor problems you may want the advice of your pediatrician, psychologist, or school counselor. This book is not a substitute for the assistance of _____ persons.

Answer Key

1. strengthen
2. competing
3. reinforce
4. weaken
   desirable
5. temper tantrums
6. temper tantrum
7. temper tantrums *or* problem behaviors
8. temper tantrum *or* problem behavior
9. consistent
10. praise *or* hug
    reinforce
11. temper tantrums
12. many
13. simple
14. strengthened *or* strong
15. social
    nonsocial
16. reinforcement
17. program
18. money *or* toys *or* points for a trip, etc.
19. count *or* graph
20. strengthening *or* reinforcing
21. end
22. social reinforcers
23. professional

Section 3
Normal Problems, Normal Children

Most parents of normal children have problems of some kind. This section describes some problems that parents of normal preschool children say they often have. For each problem we have included a unit that outlines the specific steps to take for bringing about the behavior change. The notion is that the parents can go directly to these units without even reading the rest of the book. On the other hand, we believe that if parents do read this book, they can eventually design their own programs when problems arise.

We have currently field tested only a small number of these cookbook type units (Forgatch and Toobert, in preparation). Our studies show that they work for most parents. As we do more studies, more units will be added to later revisions of the book. Eventually this section should contain 20 or more units dealing with the major concerns that normal parents have about bringing up their children.

10
Noncompliance

There are some children who, as they get older, seem to have a one-word vocabulary: "No." Noncompliance is a term for children who refuse to obey, who say "No" all the time. "Eat your potatoes, Johnny." As his mother says this, Johnny pushes his plate farther away. This parent has to ask 5 or 6 times before the child will even start. He also has to be asked to hang up his coat 5 or 6 times before he responds. By not hanging up his coat he can control his mother's attention for 5 or 10 minutes. This reinforces him for being negativistic.*

Noncompliance "works." It effectively teaches people to stop asking you to do things. Each request leads to arguments, or has to be repeated 5 or 6 times. This punishment teaches people to stop asking you to do things.

Count the number of requests and commands you give for an hour or so each day for 3 days. Also mark each time the child noncomplies. If you repeat your request 4 times before he gets around to washing his face, that is 3 noncompliances.

---

* We wish to thank Marion Forgatch and Debbie Toobert for field testing this material.

Steps to Take:

1. Buy a box of colored stars. Tape a graph like the one below to the refrigerator door.

GOLD STAR CHART

Name _Timothy_   Date _7/19 – 7/25_

M	T	W	Th	F	S	S
★★ ★ ★ ★	★★ ★ ★★	★				

A gold star means _no noncomplies for one hour._

Behaviors	M	T	W	Th	F	S	S
Requests	⊬⊬⊬ I	⊬⊬⊬	III	II			
Noncomplies	III	IIII	I				

2. Explain to your child: "You do a lot of nice things, and I appreciate that, but there is a problem that bothers me. Most of the time you forget to mind. I'm going to help you practice so that you'll remember to mind better. See this chart here on the door? Each time you mind you can put a star in the box. When you have earned _____ stars, you get to have a special reward. Every time you forget to mind, I'm going to put a line in the box, like this. How many stars do you think you will get today?"

3. Each time your child does comply, give him his star immediately. Show him how pleased you are. Say to him "That's great! When I asked you to _____ , you did it right away. What a *big boy* (*girl*) you are! Should I put up the star, or would you like to?" Be as enthusiastic as you can. Sometimes give him a hug or a kiss as well.

4. You have an idea of how many times a day your child minds from the chart you kept last week. If he minds 5 times a day, on the average, set a goal of 5 stars that must be earned on the first day to get a special reward. After a few days, set a goal of 6, and so on. You start where your child is and gradually make it a little bit harder to earn a reward. Some suggestions for rewards are given below. You may have some ideas of your own to add. Ask your child. He may know best what he'd like to work for.

Suggestions for rewards: extra time reading to your child; time spent doing something of your child's choice; cookies, raisins, pennies. Another idea is the grab bag. Go to the store and buy several small items of the party variety: jacks, small rubber balls, rubber snakes and spiders, marbles, play rings, bubbles, etc. Wrap them up and put them in a bag. If your child earns his stars for the day, he gets a chance to pull one thing out of the grab bag.

5. Explain to your child what will happen each time he forgets to mind by saying, "Each time you forget to mind, you will have 2 minutes of Time Out. That means you go to the bathroom like this." (Get up and walk with the child, open the door to the bathroom, and have him go in.) "I will set this timer for 2 minutes. When it rings, you can come out." Here's how Time Out works (see Chapter 8 for more details):
   a. Time Out means 2 minutes alone in the bathroom with the door closed.
   b. Your child is sent to Time Out each time he forgets to mind. You say "Tim, you forgot to mind. Go to Time Out." Don't argue or nag. If he does not comply, he is reminded that he must spend an extra minute for not going alone.
   c. The kitchen timer is set so your child can hear it ring when time is up.
   d. Nobody talks to your child while in Time Out under any circumstances.
   e. If your child is noisy when the timer rings, reset the timer for an additional minute, and he stays in Time Out. You may have to do this a number of times until he is quiet.
   f. Your child should clean up any mess he makes while in Time Out.

Your ability to be consistent will determine the success of your program. From now on *each* time you ask your child to do something, you have a job, too. If your child complies, you reward him. If he noncomplies, you follow through with Time Out. Before you ask him to do something, make sure it's worth your effort.

Sometimes part of the problem involves the way you ask your child to do something. Here are some pointers for making effective requests.

1. State your request clearly so that your child knows *exactly* what you expect of him. The command "Be careful with your milk," does not tell him *how* to do it. A better command would be "Don't put your glass on the edge of the table," or "Please put your glass in the center of the table."

2. Don't rely on standing house rules when you tell your child to do something. Preschoolers are still too young to remember. Restate the rule. For example, "Remember the furniture," could be more effectively stated by saying "Remember, don't put your feet on the furniture," or "Please take your feet off the furniture."

3. Make your requests politely. You know how much more likely you are to respond when someone says "Please."

4. Give your child enough time to comply before you use Time Out.

11
So Your Child Teases

If your three- to six-year-old does any of the following about once an hour, you have a "teaser" on your hands: calls names and makes faces; provokes, irritates and interrupts other children as they play; or has loud yelling matches about who "owns" something or whose turn it is. Most young children may be expected to do these kinds of things once or twice a day.*

If you decide to teach your child to cut down on teasing, buy a box of gold stars, and tape the gold star chart to your refrigerator door. *Write down on the chart the specific things your child does* that are teases. Pick the things he does at least once a day or more as your "target" (see page 76).

Explain the program to your child. "There is a lot of teasing going on. I'm going to help you practice so it won't happen so often. See the chart here on the door? Each time a tease happens, I'm going to put a mark in the box. Each day has its own box; see, here is one for today. If you go a whole hour with no teases, then you get a gold star in the box. How many stars do you think you will get today?"

Do not nag or scold when he teases. Simply say "That's a tease!" *Do not argue or debate* with him. Just put a check in the square for that day and that hour. Record it each time in as calm a

* We particularly wish to thank Matt Fleischman for pilot testing this program.

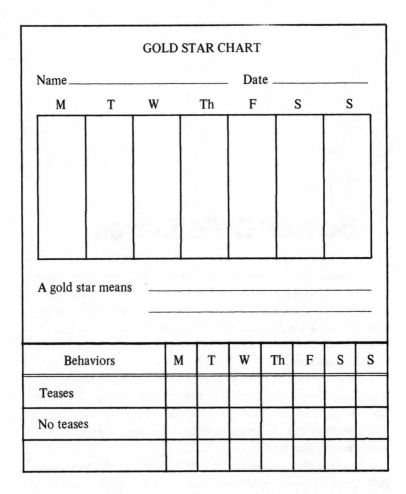

GOLD STAR CHART

Name_____ Date _____

M	T	W	Th	F	S	S

A gold star means _____

_____

Behaviors	M	T	W	Th	F	S	S
Teases							
No teases							

voice as you can. When he has been home for an hour with no teases, say "Hey, it has really been nice. No teases for an hour! What a big boy (girl) you are! Should I put the gold star up or do you want to do it?" Give him the star even if he has been watching TV alone and not playing with anyone. Be as enthusiastic as you can!

For many teasers, the gold star approval game is all that is necessary.

Explain to your child what will happen each time he forgets not to tease by saying, "Each time you forget and fight or tease, you will have 2 minutes of Time Out. That means you go to the bathroom

76

like this." (Get up and walk with the child, open the door to the bathroom, and have him go in.) "I will set this timer for 2 minutes. When it rings, you can come out." Here's how Time Out works (see Chapter 8 for more details):

a. Time Out means 2 minutes alone in the bathroom with the door closed.

b. Your child is sent to Time Out each time he forgets and teases or fights. You say "Tim, you forgot and teased. Go to Time Out." Don't argue or nag. If he does not comply, he is reminded that he must spend an extra minute for not going alone.

c. The kitchen timer is set so your child can hear it ring when time is up.

d. Nobody talks to your child while in Time Out under any circumstances.

e. If your child is noisy when the timer rings, reset the timer for an additional minute, and he stays in Time Out. You may have to do this a number of times until he is quiet.

f. Your child should clean up any mess made while in Time Out.

12
Toilet Training
Three-Year-Olds

When the normal child is twenty-four months or older, he can learn to stay dry. But you have to teach him. Generally, you can teach him to do this in about 2 or 3 weeks.

Tape the gold star chart (page 70) to the refrigerator door. Buy a pair of training pants and a box of gold stars and then explain the program to him. "I'm going to help you practice staying dry. Every time you go to the bathroom, you get a gold star on your chart. You also get a snack. Why don't you go to the potty right now?"

If the child refuses to go to the bathroom, do not force him, do not nag or scold. If he does go, even a little bit, then say something like, "That's good!" Be enthusiastic. "Now we put a gold star on the chart, like so. What would you like for your snack today?"

At dinner in the evening, announce to his father how many times the child went to the toilet. On those days when he manages to stay dry, take a crayon and write a large D at the bottom of the column for that day, and make sure that this is also announced at the dinner table.

When the child forgets and wets his pants, have him immediately rinse the pants out in the sink and put them in the dryer. Have a sponge right there in the bathroom so that he can clean up any mess he makes on the floor by spilling water and soap. Do this every time he wets his pants.

Do not nag or scold: Be calm. "Oh, oh! You forgot and wet your pants. OK, let's go into the bathroom and I'll show you how to wash them."

Put some water in the basin, take soap and lightly soap the pants and scrub them, and then let him finish the task. When he spills water on the floor, show him how to mop it up with a sponge. Show him how to rinse the pants and then how to put them in the dryer. "OK, now you have to wait until the pants are dry because you only have one pair, so you'll sit here and wait. I'll see you in a little while. Bye-bye."

13
Bed-Wetting: A Simple First Approach

The problem of nighttime wetting for children four years and older is one that is encountered by many parents. Some parents seem to be able to train their child to stay dry with little or no difficulty. For others, the learning seems to be difficult. We believe that part of the difference in effectiveness lies in the kind of program used by parents. The program outlined here is a simple one, one that you might try first. If this program does not bring an end to the bed-wetting, then other methods should be tried.*

The child is told that wetting the bed at night is a problem. "Now that you are a big girl, it is time to learn to stop wetting the bed at night. I'll bet you would like to learn how to stop that, wouldn't you? Yes, and then we wouldn't have to wash the sheets every morning. I'm going to help you practice so you can stop wetting the bed. OK? What would you like to earn while you practice? You will be able to earn something each day."

Make a list of inexpensive, readily available reinforcers she would enjoy, for example, extra cereal snacks, gold stars, 10 minutes of reading to her just before bedtime. The child should be told that if she remains dry during the night, she will get the reinforcers the very next day. For the first week, reinforcers should be administered daily, every other day the second week,

---

* We wish to thank Elizabeth Steinboch for her assistance in field testing an earlier version of the program.

every fourth or fifth day the third week, and so on until the reinforcers are phased out. Post the gold star chart (page 70) and place a gold star for each dry night. When the child stays dry for a night, announce it at the dinner table with a special hat, a tiny cake with a candle, anything to make it fun for her and the entire family.

When she wets the bed, have her change her own bedding. No lectures—do not scold! Have her put the wet clothing and sheets in the laundry room. Remember, her progress will be uneven. At first, she will have a dry night and many wet nights. Over a period of weeks, this will change and she will wet only occasionally. Keep her on the program until she has been dry for several weeks.

14
Temper Tantrums

Many parents seem to be troubled with children who have frequent temper tantrums. Telling the child that he cannot have or do something often results in loud whining, yelling, running, hitting, and throwing things. This display may last from a minute or two up to half an hour's harassment of the parent. There are perhaps some good days, but on a bad day tantrums may occur 2 or 3 times. Tantrums can occur in the supermarket, at the playground, or in the home of a relative. Some children seem to have a sixth sense about selecting the most embarrassing situations in which to stage their performances. It comes to a point for some parents where they are afraid to say "No" to their child. Collect data each day for a week to get a baseline rate.*

The basic idea is to teach the child that temper tantrums and whining will no longer "work." Arrange for a conference with your child. Both parents must be present. "You are a big girl (boy) now, and can do lots of things. One problem though is a worry to your mother and me. It seems a lot of times when we say 'No' you get pretty upset and do lots of yelling and whining. I think you can learn to stop doing that; we will help you practice. Each time you have a temper tantrum, we will say, 'OK, 2 minutes of Time Out.' Then you go into the bathroom. I will set this timer for 2 minutes. When it goes off, you come out. OK?"

* We wish to thank Brian Danaher for his assistance in field testing these procedures.

Remember that Time Out (TO) means 2 minutes alone in the bathroom with the door closed. The child is put in Time Out at the start of each tantrum behavior. If she does not go into Time Out when she is supposed to, she is told that she must spend an extra minute in TO for not minding. The kitchen timer is set so the child can hear it ring when TO is over, and under no circumstances does anyone talk to the child during TO.

If the child is noisy when the timer rings, the timer is reset for one minute and the child remains in Time Out. This is done as many times as is needed until the child is quiet when the timer rings. The child must clean up any mess she made while in TO.

It is also a good idea to use the gold star chart (page 70) and provide gold stars for each compliance. If you say "No" and she minds you with no whines and temper tantrums, say "Hey, I said 'No' and you acted like a big girl (boy)! That's great! Here's a gold star for your chart." The temper tantrums should reduce by at least half by the end of 2 or 3 weeks. If not, then consult a trained behavior modifier for assistance.

If she has her temper tantrum at the store or somewhere else, then put her in Time Out when she gets home.

15
The Midnight Intruder

Many parents find it is a warm, pleasant feeling to have their two-year-old occasionally slip into their bed in the middle of the night. Certainly this is not a "problem" behavior. Some difficulties seem to arise, however, when the parents decide that it is time to teach the child to stay in his own bed. The following procedure seems to work well, and is a nice example of the simplicity of some social learning programs.

Be sure both parents agree that they want privacy. Both parents then explain the program to their child. "Now that you are a big boy (girl), it is time for you to learn to stay in your own bed at night. When you forget and climb in our bed, we are just going to take you back to your own bed."

"If you stay in your own bed all night, then one of us will climb into *your* bed in the morning and read stories for 15 minutes. OK? If you climb in our bed, no stories. If you stay in your bed, then we'll come there in the morning for story time."

If the child cries when you return him to his bed, ignore him and let him cry it out. He should be able to learn to stay in bed after 3 or 4 more attempts to invade yours.

Use the gold star chart (page 70). When he stays in his bed, be sure to announce to everyone what a "big boy (girl)" he (or she) is. Brag about it to friends and relatives when he can hear you.

16
Whining

Most children whine once or twice a day to get attention, or over some minor injury, or when you leave. But a child who whines once an hour or more may present a behavior problem. If you want to reduce your child's rate of whining, you must teach the child that whining will no longer "work." To do this, you will need to change the way that you respond when he whines.*

Buy a box of gold stars, and tape a gold star chart to the refrigerator door. Explain the program to your child. "You are a big boy (girl) now and can do a lot of things. There is a problem, though, that bothers me. The problem is that you whine a lot. I'm going to help you practice so this won't happen so often. See the chart here on the door? Each time you whine, I'm going to put a mark in the box. Each day has its own box. See, here is for today. If you go a whole hour with no whines, then you get to have a gold star in the box. (See page 88.) How many stars do you think you will get today?"

---

* We wish to thank Marion Forgatch and Ed Monnig for field testing this program.

GOLD STAR CHART

Name_____ Date _____

M	T	W	Th	F	S	S

A gold star means _____

_____

Behaviors	M	T	W	Th	F	S	S
Whines							
No whines							

Explain to your child what will happen each time he forgets and whines by saying, "Each time you forget and whine, you will have 2 minutes of Time Out. That means you go to the bathroom like this." (Get up and walk with the child, open the door to the bathroom and have him go in.) "I'll set this timer for 2 minutes. When it rings, you can come out." Here's how Time Out works (see Chapter 8 for more details):

    a. Time Out means 2 minutes alone in the bathroom with the door closed.

b. Your child is sent to Time Out each time he (she) forgets not to whine. You say "Bill, you forgot not to whine. Go to Time Out." Don't argue or nag. If he does not comply, he is reminded that he must spend an extra minute for not going alone.

c. The kitchen timer is set so your child can hear it ring when time is up.

d. Nobody talks to your child while in Time Out under any circumstances.

e. If your child is noisy when the timer rings, reset the timer for an additional minute, and he stays in Time Out. You may have to do this a number of times until he is quiet.

f. Your child should clean up any mess made while in Time Out.

After a week or two, let the child use his stars to "buy" extra reading time or extra snuggling time before bed. Another idea is a "grab bag." Buy some penny things he likes and put them in a sack. If he gets a gold star for that morning, he gets to take one thing out of the bag. The whines should reduce by *at least half* their usual rate at the end of 2 or 3 weeks.

17
To Bed or Not to Bed

You tuck him in bed, kiss him goodnight, and what happens? Five minutes later you hear tiny footsteps in the hall, a little voice calling . . . . If this happens almost every night, you may want to change these behaviors.

Begin by explaining the program to your child after you tuck him in. "You just went to the potty and had a drink of water. Is there anything else you need right now? OK, from now on I want you to stay in your bed after I tuck you in. If you get out of bed, then you go into Time Out for 2 minutes. If you stay in bed and are quiet, then tomorrow night you and I will have a special treat. I will read to you for 10 minutes before you go to bed. If you get out of bed, then you get Time Out and no bedtime story. If you stay in bed, then tomorrow night is story time and you get a gold star for your chart." (See page 70.)

If the child stays in bed but asks for you, and you are sure he is OK, then ignore him. When he gets out of bed, use Time Out. Do not lecture. Explain to your child what will happen each time he forgets and gets out of bed by saying, "Each time you forget and get out of bed, you will have 2 minutes of Time Out. That means you go to the bathroom like this." (Get up and walk with the child, open the door to the bathroom, and have him go in.) "I'll set this timer for 2 minutes. When it rings, you can come out."

Here's how Time Out works (see Chapter 8 for more details):

a. Time Out means 2 minutes alone in the bathroom with the door closed.

b. Your child is sent to Time Out each time he (she) forgets and gets out of bed. You say "Mike, you forgot and got out of bed. Go to Time Out." Don't argue or nag. If he does not comply, he is reminded that he must spend an extra minute for not going alone.

c. The kitchen timer is set so your child can hear it ring when time is up.

d. Nobody talks to your child while in Time Out under any circumstances.

e. If your child is noisy when the timer rings, reset the timer for an additional minute, and he stays in Time Out. You may have to do this a number of times until he is quiet.

f. Your child should clean up any mess made while in Time Out.

The next night, give the child a 30-minute warning. "Half an hour to bedtime, better pick up your things and get ready." If the child stayed in bed the previous night, even if he cried all night long, say "You stayed in bed last night so you get a gold star on your chart and we get to read a story as soon as you are in bed. Are you all ready?"

If the child didn't stay in bed the night before, say "We don't get a bedtime story tonight. Think you can stay in bed tonight?" *Do not* lecture or scold.

By the end of 2 or 3 weeks, this program should have the child staying in bed almost every night. Be sure to brag to friends what a big boy (girl) he (or she) is and show them the gold star chart.

If your problem is a relatively simple one, you've probably been able to use the procedures described in this chapter to reduce the problem by at least half.

Section 4
Problem Children

When the Social Learning Project began in the mid 1960's, the mission was to help families of aggressive children. In the process, we had to learn a great deal about normal families, too. But this section outlines the steps to be followed by parents who have children with *severe* problems. These are children who are referred for professional help because their acting out behavior disrupts the lives of parents, teachers, friends, siblings, and peers alike. We assume, therefore, that the parent is working with a well-trained behavior therapist. In our own work, we began treatment by having the parents read this book while working with a professional. For these severe problems, you might wish to listen to the cassette tapes which give examples of the many things that can go awry in trying to use these ideas to help children who are really skilled at being aggressive (Patterson & Forgatch, 1975, 1976).

These steps are based upon our experience in working with over 100 families of problem children. The outcome and follow-up studies have been published in many books and scientific journals (Patterson, 1975a, 1975b; Patterson, Reid, Jones & Conger, 1975; Reid & Patterson, 1976; Patterson, 1976; Arnold, Levine & Patterson, 1975). We continue to work with both problem and normal families in order to increase our understanding.

18
The Coercive Child

The coercive child makes other people uncomfortable. *All* children do this *some* of the time. The problem child does it about once every 2 or 3 minutes. Much of what he does are little things: he may whine a lot, yell, cry, break things, put others down, argue, yell, hit, throw things, or just run over the furniture. People have trouble trying to relax around such a child.

About half of these children also have trouble getting along in school. They do the same things there, too: yelling, running around, not minding, and sometimes fighting. Other children tend not to like them and they often do not do well in their studies.

The pattern has usually been there for quite awhile. For a long time you kid yourself into thinking he will outgrow it. He doesn't. Basically he goes right on making people miserable. The only thing that changes over the years are the means by which he does it. These children are usually labeled as out-of-control, aggressive, or hyperactive.

1. The labels are not important; the fact is that parents can be trained to be effective in changing about 2 out of 3 of these children. In this type of treatment, it is the _____ who work with the child, not the doctors.

2. If there are 2 parents, or 2 adults in the family, *both* of them must work together. If just one parent tries to change the child without the other *equally sharing* the work, then this treatment will likely _____. Sometimes even 2 parents working together are hardly enough.

3. Remember, this child has had *years* of practice and training in being a monster. He was trained by the family. He learned that being coercive really works in turning off unpleasant things that come up in the family. If your mother asks you to help with the dishes, yell, argue, or be sloppy. All of these things will make it so unpleasant that she will stop asking you to help. Studies show that most of these children do _____ do chores, and that is how they manage to get out of it.

4. If somebody in the family teases them, they hit, or yell until the teasing is stopped. These kids know that pain control really _____ .

   If you want something, take it. If you want your mother to stay home instead of going to the movies, then just make it so painful that she will give it up. Crying works, yelling helps; being nasty to the baby-sitter, breaking things, having a temper tantrum—all of these are techniques for teaching people what to do.

5. Basically the child does what *he* wants to do. One thing that these children have in common is that if you ask them to do something, there is a very good chance that they will_____ do it. Noncompliance is a key part of this approach. Therefore, it is almost always a part of the first treatment steps.

6. Teaching a child to mind once in awhile is, of course, something we generally work on with two-, three-, and four-year-olds. That in fact is your basic problem. You must train a child eight, nine, or ten years old who has really only begun to be a person. Most coercive children are really very

    _____ .

7. You would think that getting their way as much as they do that these children would be pretty happy, friendly, warm kids. They generally are not. More likely you get the feeling of their being irritable, sad, moody, with a chip on their shoulders. Many parents say that he is not a warm, friendly child either. We've been fascinated over the years in seeing that when the parents teach the family to stop using pain control, then these children become _____ warm and affectionate!

    If you have such a child, and you want to change some of the things he does, we assume you have a trained behavior therapist to work with and that you have read the first part of this book. Reading the book and listening to the cassettes will help you understand what your therapist is doing. He will help you set up your first programs. But our hunch is that the more you as a parent know, the more likely you can eventually set up your own programs. So the first thing, then, is to read this book or one like it.

8. Next, you should pinpoint one or two of the unpleasant behaviors that must be changed. Start with problems that occur at least 2 or 3 times a _____ .

9. Noncomply is a good one for most of these children. The problem is for you to spell out what kind of behavior problem he *does*. Count it only when you have given a clear command. If he argues, then say "That is a noncomply," and mark it down. If he dawdles and takes longer than a half a minute, then that's a _____ .

You should only have to ask once and expect the child to mind about 3 times out of 4. Take an hour during the day when he is home and give him 4 or 5 *clear* requests, for example, "Stop teasing," "Please go outside and play." Collect this kind of data on your chart for 3 or 4 days. Now you are ready to begin your program.

Name *Billy*			Date 8/16 – 8/22				
Behavior	M	T	W	Th	F	S	S
Noncomply	‖‖|	‖‖	‖‖‖‖ ‖	‖‖‖			
Comply	‖	‖	O	‖‖‖‖			
Total points	-3	-2	-7	2			

If he hasn't already seen it, show the child your chart. Give him the following instructions:

> "You do some pretty nice things around here, but one of the things you do that bothers your dad and me is that you are not very good at minding. We are going to help you practice that. When we ask you to do something and you do it, then I'll put a mark down here (comply). If you forget and argue or don't mind within a half a minute or so, then you get a mark here (noncomply). You also go to Time Out. We'll come back to that in a minute. At the end of the day, if you have more points here (comply) than here (noncom-

ply), then you can stay up 30 minutes longer, or something like that. What would you like to work for when you practice minding?"

10. Many of the children will refuse to work for anything and try to talk you out of using the program. Don't argue with them; go ahead and set a consequence which he can earn each night. Later on he will negotiate with you. Pick something simple, for example, a special dessert, reading to him for 10 minutes, playing cards with him, etc. In addition, use a hug, praise or some social _____ when he has a good day.

11. Now you should explain Time Out to him. If possible, role play it with him. Read the material in Chapter 8 on what to say and how to do it. You might also listen to the cassette tapes on Time Out and Noncompliance. Above all, do _____ argue, do _____ try to make him "explain" why he doesn't mind. He does not know why. Your lectures make things worse.

12. It is important that both parents take turns in the practice sessions. One day the mother does it for an hour. The next day the _____ does it. If only one parent does it, the child will soon figure that out.

13. After the first week, the program goes into effect all day long. If the father comes home and sees the child noncomply, he should take over and _____ it, and put the child in _____ _____.

14. Remember to change the back-up reinforcer every few
_____. Some parents use the point system as a way for
the child to earn his weekly allowance. If his allowance is 50
cents a week, then his contract is set up so that he *could* earn
50 points by behaving very well. Each point, then, is worth
one _____ . That is a pretty hefty salary. Later on
you can shift the program so that he earns his allowance by
doing chores each week.

15. Even in the first week you might add some things he can do
to make things better for the family. A good item here would
be chores, for example, make his bed, clean up his bedroom,
wash the dishes, sweep, take out the garbage. Give him a daily
chore to do. Each chore that is done properly would give him
_____ . Remember to tell him when he does a good
job: "Your room was nice and clean today. There's a point
for that." If his work was sloppy, calmly tell him what was
wrong and give no points.

After a week or two of this, you should have the noncompliance and chore problems pretty well in hand. He should be going
into Time Out pretty well. You should be spanking and yelling less.
Your practice period is over; now you can add 2 more problems, for
example, yelling, teasing, interrupting, whining, wandering.
Your contract changes now. Each item on it now has a point
price tag. It would look like this.

100

Behavior	Points	M	T	W	Th	F	S	S
Comply	1	6	2	9				
Chores	5	3	5	0				
Tease	-1	-2	-4	-2				
Whine	-1	-5	-3	-1				
Total points:		2	0	6				
Each point earns 1 penny								

Name _Billy_   Date _12/6 – 12/12_

16. Each comply earns _____ point. Chores done perfectly earn _____ points; if less than perfect, then you set the amount.

17. Tease and whine are different. Each time they occur, it costs the child a point *and* he also goes to _____ _____ . Give him enough requests each day (5 or 10) so that he can pile up a number of points by complying. You might want to add some other point earning items, such as 5 points for coming home on time from school, extra points for extra chores. If you have put it together right, most days should wind up with him earning points. Too many days ending in zero or minus means you should _____ the contract.

   If you are getting too many minus days, then drop one or two of the point cost items, such as whine. Continue to use Time Out (see Chapter 8) for whine, but he loses no points for it.

18. At the end of each day, go over his performance. Remember, _____ lectures and _____ put downs. "You had a pretty good day today. You got 6 points for minding, 3 points for doing a good job on your bedroom. You lost 2 points for teasing and 5 for whining."

19. You should write on the contract what the points earn. For example, it could be that 10 points means he can stay up 30 minutes later that night; 5 points means he gets his special dessert. Zero points means he goes to bed 30 minutes early; minus 10 points means he goes to bed right after supper. You set these consequences after talking it over with your _____. This is also something you continue to change every few days.

20. About half of these children have difficulties in school as well as at home. This means that you and your therapist will eventually go to the school and negotiate some further changes in the contract. The child is given a card which he gives to his teacher at the end of the day and she initials it. If any of the problem behaviors occur, she places a check beside that item, for example, yell, fight, out of chair, homework not done. Each of these checks means a loss of _____ for his program.

21. What usually happens is he "forgets" his card. This, too, has a consequence, for example, 5 points off for a lost card. Your reaction to each problem situation should be to set a _____.

22. If his grades are poor, you might set up a place where he can work quietly at home. Provide him with points for 30 minutes of homework each day. At first, do not require that his work be accurate in order to earn points. If you look at his homework, and you should, do _____ criticize. Find *something* about it to _____.

After a month or two, things should begin to be more peaceful. Usually coercive children have brothers and sisters who are also out of control. As you get time and energy, you might set up a program for them, too.

23. Remember, as crises come up, you should set a
   _____ . If he tears up the neighbor's fence, then
   provide some natural consequence, for example, he fixes it, or
   he earns money by mowing lawns to pay for it.

As he comes under normal social controls, you can stop using the contract and rely upon social consequences and his allowance. You will also find that he is warmer and happier. The sadness and moodiness usually drop away, too.

24. You should practice something which will facilitate this
   process. Each day one parent should spend 10 minutes listening. Take turns doing it. Start it by asking him about something he did that day. Then simply _____ to what
   he says.

25. Do _____ criticize. Just *listen*. Ask him a few questions
   to let him know you are really interested. Look at him while
   he is talking. Many parents say this child won't talk to them; at
   first yours won't either. He will expect you to either put him
   down, or to get bored with what he is saying. At first he may
   only talk for a minute or two.

26. That's fine! Listen, for example, _____ it. Talk time
   like this is a good way to bring the two of you back together,
   and that of course is what it is really all about.

Answer Key

1. parents
2. fail
3. not
4. works *or* turns off unpleasant events
5. not
6. young *or* little kids *or* immature
7. more
8. day
9. noncomply
10. reinforcer
11. not
    not
12. father
13. mark
    Time Out
14. days
    penny
15. points
16. one (1)
    five (5)
17. Time Out
    change
18. no
    no
19. child
20. points
21. consequence
22. not
    reinforce *or* praise
23. consequence
24. listen
25. not
26. reinforce

19
The Child Who Steals

1. Most children steal once or twice in their lives. But if you live with a child who you suspect steals once a month or more, then he is a problem child and you should _____ him to stop stealing. The problem is serious. Studies show the high rate stealer is the one who is likely to end up in our institutions later on.

2. When he gets caught by an eye witness, it is no problem to count it. However, be sure to include in your counting (a) when he borrows things without asking; (b) money missing from your purse; (c) when anyone says they saw him steal; (d) when he shows up with some new item he says he found or was given to him. This way there will be times when you are not "fair." Do _____ try to prove he stole something. That is the trap employed by most children who steal. You will probably end up punishing him for things he didn't do, but he will learn then to stay out of any situation where it might look like he is stealing.

3. There are two problems that often go with stealing: wandering and lying. Most children who steal are allowed to spend a great deal of time roaming around unsupervised by adults. They are often out late at night, sometimes overnight. Most of the weekend they are off on their own. You will have to teach him to spend more time at home and to tell you where he is going and to return on time. If he _____ less, then there is less chance for him to steal.

There are a small number who do not wander about stealing from the community. They steal mainly from their parents. You might try the program listed here but it is more likely that training in parent-child negotiation would work better. The book *Families* (Patterson, 1971, 1975) describes such procedures. The problem there is not so much a child given more freedom than he can handle, but instead a battle between parent and child.

When beginning your program, first tell your child that you are tracking and counting when (a) things are missing, (b) new things show up, (c) people say he stole something, or (d) you are sure he stole something.

4. Count these for about 2 weeks. At the end of that time, tell him that any one of these means he does at least one hour of work. Even if the stealing cannot be *proven*, he gets an hour of _____.

5. If the stolen item is expensive, add more _____time.

6. If he stole something from a neighbor or a store, then he must work *and* return the item and offer to _____ for them.

7. Set up a contract which also includes lying and wandering. A lie costs 5 points. Work out how long it should take for him to get home from school. Give him 2 points for getting home on time *and* letting you know, for example, "Hi, Mom, I'm home." He loses one point for every minute that he is_____ .

8. When he is home, he should ask permission to go somewhere and tell you who he will be with and when he will be back, for example, "Dad, I'm going over to the hangout for an hour with Jim. Be back at six." For asking permission, he gets 2 points. For coming home on time, he gets another 2 points. This means that when he leaves the yard he should ask _____ .

Use of a chart like the one shown below is helpful.

Name Sam				Date 11/22 – 11/28			
Behaviors	M	T	W	Th	F	S	S
Steal (-10)	No	No	-10	No			
Home from school (2)	2	2	0	0			
Lie (-5)	No	-5	-5	No			
Asks to go (2)	2	2,2 2	0	0			
Home on time (2)	2	2	0	0			
Chores	10	5	10	0			
Total.	16	10	-15	0			
Points = 1 penny for allowance Steal = 1 hour work							

9. Set an early curfew for him. During the first week he can be out on the street only one night and then he must be back by 8 o'clock. If he comes in late, he loses _____ points from the contract *and* gets a work detail. Not coming home when he's supposed to is the key to the whole thing. Help him learn *to do* what he says he will do or agrees to do. For this reason, when he does not live up to his word, come down hard, for example, point loss plus work.

10. If he does well in the first week, then let him go on the street one weekday night (until eight or nine o'clock) and one weekend night (until nine or ten o'clock). Again, see that he comes home on time. If he steals or gets into trouble, then begin all over, for example, one night out or even a week with _____ nights out.

Put up a list of chores and give a number of points to be earned for each; below is an example:

Clean own room	2
Mow lawn	20
Take out garbage	1
Sweep garage	3
Wash car	15
Wash windows	50
Pull weeds	20
Paint fence	50
Clean toilet bowl	15
Scrub floor	15
Run errand	5
Baby-sit	20

11. Be sure that he is no longer making money from his street ac-
    tivities, for example, from selling things he steals. The idea is
    that he must now _____ the money or allowance he gets.

12. Encourage the family and relatives _____ to give him
    money for any reason. Any money he has, he must _____ .
    This is another way of teaching him to grow up.

13. As he stays out of trouble, he earns more time away from
    home. But even then the parent has the right to (*must*) know
    where he is and who he is with. It is a good idea to check on
    this information *often* at first, for example, call Jim's mother.
    If he is out and can't get back on time, he should _____
    you. You are the two people in the world who must monitor
    what the child does. No one else can do it for you. If you don't,
    he will slip into running with a bunch of kids and *they* will
    teach him.

About half the children who steal are also socially aggressive,
that is, they yell, tease, hit, argue, noncomply, and so forth. If that is
true for your child, then read the chapter on the coercive child
(Chapter 18) and add those items to your contract.

About ninety percent of the time the stealing and wandering
will stop (Reid & Patterson, 1976). It should take anywhere from 4
weeks to 4 months. Gradually remove the point system. However,
retain 2 components: (1) Each time he steals (and he *will* try again),
set a work consequence; (2) Have him do regular chores to earn his
allowance.

14. Remember, when he goofs, set a natural_____.
    Any normal child will make a serious mistake once in awhile.
    When it happens, ask him what he would consider to be a fair
    consequence. If he comes in at 1 a.m., when it should have been
    midnight, then sit down and talk about what the consequence
    should be, for example, washing dishes for 3 days, being
    grounded for a week, etc.

15. Remember, in doing this, do not _____. Tell the child
    only once why you are concerned. As he gets older, you will
    have to learn to negotiate what is fair. That is another matter.
    The book *Families* (Patterson, 1971, 1975), has some material
    on that. Several of the cassette tapes also deal with that process
    (Patterson & Forgatch, 1975, 1976).

16. Setting consequences for goofs and using positive reinforcers
    for desirable behavior are continuous features of being a good
    parent. Just because your child stops _____
    doesn't mean you can now forget about reinforcing him.

    Enjoy your child!

Answer Key

1. train *or* teach
2. not
3. wanders
4. work
5. work
6. work
7. late
8. permission
9. two (2)
10. no
11. earn
12. not
    earn
13. call
14. consequence
15. lecture *or* nag *or* scold *or* argue
16. stealing

References

Arnold, J., Levine, A. & Patterson, G. R. Changes in sibling behavior following family intervention. *Journal of Clinical and Consulting Psychology*, 1975, *43* (5), 683-688. (Also in C. Franks [Ed.], *Recent advances in behavior therapy*, in press.)

Bandura, A. Social learning theory of aggression. In J. F. Knutson (Ed.), *Control of aggression: Implications from basic research*. Chicago: Aldine Publishing Co., 1971.

Forgatch, M. & Toobert, D. Paper in preparation, 1976.

Patterson, G. R. *Families: Applications of social learning to family life*. Champaign, IL: Research Press Co., 1971, 1975.

Patterson, G. R. Multiple evaluations of a parent training program. In T. Thompson & W. S. Dockens III (Eds.), *Applications of behavior modification*. New York: Academic Press, 1975. (a)

Patterson, G. R. *Professional Guide for Families and Living With Children*. Champaign, IL: Research Press Co., 1975. (b)

Patterson, G. R. The aggressive child: Victim and architect of a coercive system. In L. A. Hamerlynck, L. C. Handy & E. J. Mash (Eds.), *Behavior modification and families. I. Theory and research*. New York: Brunner/Mazel, 1976.

Patterson, G. R. A three-stage functional analysis for children's coercive behaviors: A tactic for developing a performance theory. In D. Baer, B. C. Etzel & J. M. LeBlanc (Eds.), *New developments in behavioral research: Theory, methods, and applications. In honor of Sidney W. Bijou.* Hillsdale, NJ: Lawrence Erlbaum Associates, Inc., in press.

Patterson, G. R. & Forgatch, M. *Family living series. Part 1.* Five cassette tapes to be used with *Living With Children* and *Families.* Champaign, IL: Research Press Co., 1975.

Patterson, G. R. & Forgatch, M. *Family living series. Part 2.* Three cassette tapes to be used with *Living With Children* and *Families.* Champaign, IL: Research Press Co., 1976.

Patterson, G. R., Reid, J. B., Jones, R. R. & Conger, R. E. *A social learning approach to family intervention. Vol. 1. Families with aggressive children.* Eugene, OR: Castalia Publishing Company, 1975.

Reid, J. B. & Patterson, G. R. The modification of aggression and stealing behavior of boys in the home setting. In E. Ribes-Inesta & A. Bandura (Eds.), *Analysis of delinquency and aggression.* Hillsdale, NJ: Lawrence Erlbaum Associates, 1976.

Rosenfeld, H. M. Approval-seeking and approval-inducing functions of verbal and non-verbal responses in the dyad. *Journal of Personality and Social Psychology,* 1966, *4,* 597-605.

Rosenfeld, H. M. Non-verbal reciprocation of approval: An experimental analysis. *Journal of Experimental Social Psychology,* 1967, *3,* 102-111.

Skinner, B. F. *Science and human behavior.* New York: Macmillan Inc., 1953.

Tavormina, J. B. Basic models of parent counseling: A critical review. *Psychological Bulletin,* 1974, *8* (11), 827-835.

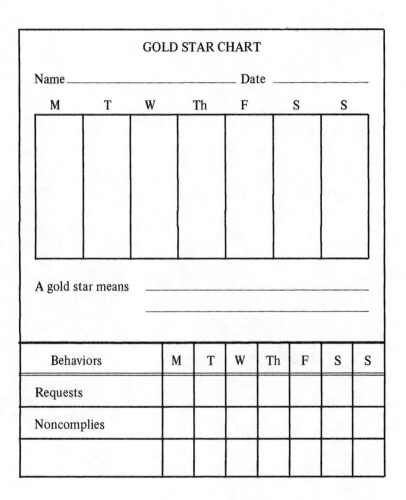

GOLD STAR CHART

Name _____ Date _____

M	T	W	Th	F	S	S

A gold star means _____

_____

Behaviors	M	T	W	Th	F	S	S
Requests							
Noncomplies							

GOLD STAR CHART

Name_____ Date _____

M	T	W	Th	F	S	S

A gold star means _____

_____

Behaviors	M	T	W	Th	F	S	S
Requests							
Noncomplies							

GOLD STAR CHART

Name_____ Date _____

M	T	W	Th	F	S	S

A gold star means _____

_____

Behaviors	M	T	W	Th	F	S	S
Requests							
Noncomplies							